Produced with the assistance of The Livingstone Corporation
(www.LivingstoneCorp.com). Project staff includes Christopher D.
Hudson, Peter Gregory and Mary Horner Collins.

Requests for information should be addressed to:
Inspirio, The gift group of Zondervan
Grand Rapids, MI 49530
http://www.inspiriogifts.com

Project Manager: Tom Dean
Design Manager: Val Buick
Cover and Interior Design: UDG | DesignWorks, Sisters, OR

Printed in China
05 06 07/CTC/6 5 4 3

trueimages

from the NIV Bible

for *Teen girls*

Ψ
inspirio™

contents

attitude

What are you like when you first wake up in the morning? Do you drag your crabby self out of bed and snap at your mom and brother if they try to talk to you? Is it common knowledge that everyone should steer clear of you before 10:00 A.M.? How about changing your mindset? What would your day be like if your first thoughts were of God's unfailing love and your first words to him were full of thanks? Maybe that would ease your worries and get you excited for the day. Hmmm . . . maybe you could become a morning person after all!

Stake Your
Life on It!

You just lashed out at a friend. Then you snapped at your little sister. If you've been constantly irritated with others lately, you might be overdue for your own heart check.

1 Peter 4:1

Therefore, since Christ suffered in his body, arm yourselves also with the same attitude, because he who has suffered in his body is done with sin.

Luke 6:45

Jesus said, "The good man brings good things out of the good stored up in his heart, and the evil man brings evil things out of the evil stored up in his heart. For out of the overflow of his heart his mouth speaks."

Ephesians 4:21–23

Surely you heard of him and were taught in him in accordance with the truth that is in Jesus. You were taught, with regard to your former way of life, to put off your old self, which is being corrupted by its deceitful desires; to be made new in the attitude of your minds.

✳ 1 Peter 1:13

Therefore, prepare your minds for action; be self-controlled; set your hope fully on the grace to be given you when Jesus Christ is revealed.

✳ Colossians 3:12

Therefore, as God's chosen people, holy and dearly loved, clothe yourselves with compassion, kindness, humility, gentleness and patience.

✳ Philippians 2:14–15

Do everything without complaining or arguing, so that you may become blameless and pure, children of God without fault in a crooked and depraved generation, in which you shine like stars in the universe.

Philippians 4:5

Let your gentleness be evident to all. The Lord is near.

Proverbs 15:15

All the days of the oppressed are wretched,
*   but the cheerful heart has a continual feast.*

Psalm 68:3

But may the righteous be glad
*   and rejoice before God;*
*   may they be happy and joyful.*

How many eighty-year-old models do you see on magazine covers? Even the most beautiful women eventually get old and forgotten. No matter how beautiful they once were, their beauty just doesn't last. It's fleeting—going, going, gone. You probably spend a lot of time trying to look your best. That's fine, but you also need to spend time with God so that you develop lasting beauty— the kind of character that sets you apart and doesn't fade with time. It gets better and better, making you beautiful no matter how old you are!

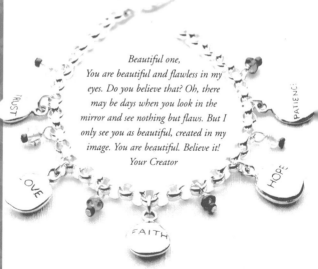

Beautiful one,
You are beautiful and flawless in my
eyes. Do you believe that? Oh, there
may be days when you look in the
mirror and see nothing but flaws. But I
only see you as beautiful, created in my
image. You are beautiful. Believe it!
Your Creator

✳ Proverbs 31:30

Charm is deceptive, and beauty is fleeting;
*   but a woman who fears the LORD is to be praised.*

✳ 1 Peter 3:3–4

Your beauty should not come from outward adornment, such as braided hair and the wearing of gold jewelry and fine clothes. Instead, it should be that of your inner self, the unfading beauty of a gentle and quiet spirit, which is of great worth in God's sight.

Isaiah 52:7

How beautiful on the mountains
   are the feet of those who bring good news,
who proclaim peace,
   who bring good tidings,
who proclaim salvation,
   who say to Zion,
"Your God reigns!"

1 Samuel 16:7

But the LORD said to Samuel, "Do not consider his
appearance or his height, for I have rejected him.
The LORD does not look at the things man looks at.
Man looks at the outward appearance, but the LORD
                    looks at the heart."

Ezekiel 28:17

Your heart became proud
   on account of your beauty,
and you corrupted your wisdom
   because of your splendor.
So I threw you to the earth;
   I made a spectacle of you
before kings.

✳ Proverbs 11:22

Like a gold ring in a pig's snout
is a beautiful woman who shows no discretion.

✳ 1 Timothy 2:9–10

I also want women to dress modestly, with decency and
propriety, not with braided hair or gold or pearls or
expensive clothes, but with good deeds, appropriate for
women who profess to worship God.

✳ Zechariah 9:16–17

The LORD their God will save them on that day
as the flock of his people.
They will sparkle in his land
like jewels in a crown.
How attractive and beautiful they will be!
Grain will make the young men thrive,
and new wine the young women.

body image

It seems like everybody wants to change something about the way they look. People put a lot of money and energy into trying to reach physical perfection. Do you want the secret to unfading beauty? It's not plastic surgery, a new makeup regimen or a trendy diet. The secret is to have your beauty come from the inside—from a gentle and quiet spirit. No matter how great your hair looks, no matter what clothing size you can squeeze into, no matter how amazing the luster of your skin is—all those things will fade away, and the beauty associated with them will, too. So focus on having a heart that is at rest and at peace with God, and you will be beautiful forever.

Dear daughter,

I don't have to tell you how much this world

values looks, clothes, physical perfection.

Not me. I look past that outer shell and see your heart—

that's where I can see real beauty.

Your heavenly Father

✳ Psalm 139:13–16

For you created my inmost being;
your knit me together in my mother's womb.
I praise you because I am fearfully and wonderfully made;
your works are wonderful,
I know that full well.
My frame was not hidden from you
when I was made in the secret place.
When I was woven together in the depths of the earth,
your eyes saw my unformed body.

✳ Proverbs 14:30

A heart at peace gives life to the body,
but envy rots the bones.

✳ Ecclesiastes 11:10

So then, banish anxiety from your heart
and cast off the troubles of your body,
for youth and vigor are meaningless.

✻ Matthew 6:25

Jesus said, "Therefore I tell you, do not worry about your life, what you will eat or drink; or about your body, what you will wear. Is not life more important than food, and the body more important than clothes?"

✻ Romans 6:12–13

Therefore do not let sin reign in your mortal body so that you obey its evil desires. Do not offer the parts of your body to sin, as instruments of wickedness, but rather offer yourselves to God, as those who have been brought from death to life; and offer the parts of your body to him as instruments of righteousness.

✳ 1 Corinthians 6:19–20

Do you not know that your body is a temple of the Holy Spirit, who is in you, whom you have received from God? You are not your own; you were bought at a price. Therefore honor God with your body.

✳ Philippians 3:20–21

But our citizenship is in heaven. And we eagerly await a Savior from there, the Lord Jesus Christ, who, by the power that enables him to bring everything under his control, will transform our lowly bodies so that they will be like his glorious body.

choices

You may get tired of hearing it, but it's true. The choices you make today will affect your future. A decision to start doing drugs could lead to a lifetime of addiction. A decision to be sexually active could lead to pregnancy, which could affect your ability to go on to college or have the career of your choice. A decision to forgive someone could result in a lifelong friendship. A decision to use sunscreen could stave off wrinkles and skin cancer. It's never too early to make good choices because even "small" decisions can have a big effect on your future. Never underestimate the value of wise choices; like the proverb says, they will be life for you (Proverbs 3:22).

Loved one,

The biggest choice is simple: life or death.

Following me or going your own way.

Live as though I don't exist and choose death.

Love and obey me and choose life. It's up to you.

Your heavenly Father

✳ Matthew 6:33

Jesus said, "But seek first his kingdom and his righteousness, and all these things will be given to you as well."

✳ Proverbs 3:5-6

Trust in the LORD with all your heart
*   and lean not on your own understanding;*
in all your ways acknowledge him,
*   and he will make your paths straight.*

✳ James 1:5

If any of you lacks wisdom, he should ask God, who gives generously to all without finding fault, and it will be given to him.

Romans 8:28

And we know that in all things God works for the good of those who love him, who have been called according to his purpose.

Philippians 2:13

For it is God who works in you to will and to act according to his good purpose.

Proverbs 1:7–9

The fear of the LORD is the beginning of knowledge,
but fools despise wisdom and discipline.
Listen, my son, to your father's instruction
and do not forsake your mother's teaching.
They will be a garland to grace your head
and a chain to adorn your neck.

Proverbs 16:16

How much better to get wisdom than gold,
*   to choose understanding rather than silver!*

Luke 10:41–42

"Martha, Martha," the Lord answered, "you are worried and upset about many things, but only one thing is needed. Mary has chosen what is better, and it will not be taken away from her."

Joshua 24:15

But if serving the LORD seems undesirable to you, then choose for yourselves this day whom you will serve, whether the gods your forefathers served beyond the River, or the gods of the Amorites, in whose land you are living. But as for me and my household, we will serve the LORD.

comfort

You may wonder why God has allowed certain difficulties into your life. Instead of asking why, ask him instead to comfort you. God comforts us in our troubles so that we can, in turn, comfort others. Think about it. It's the people who've been through the same pain who can really comfort us when we're going through something. What hard times has God allowed you to go through? Your parents' divorce? A problem at school? A poor self-image? Get comfort and strength from God, then share that with someone else who's in a similar situation. God will use you to touch someone else's life.

Beloved,

Trouble in this world comes in many different forms—

sickness, accidents, rejection, failures.

When you're in trouble, come to me. Because I love you,

my daughter, I will be with you and comfort you.

Your God and Comforter

✳ *Isaiah 40:1–2*

Comfort, comfort my people,
  says your God.
Speak tenderly to Jerusalem,
  and proclaim to her
that her hard service has been completed,
  that her sin has been paid for,
that she has received from the LORD's hand
  double for all her sins.

✳ *Psalm 23:4*

Even though I walk
  through the valley of the shadow of death,
I will fear no evil,
  for you are with me;
your rod and your staff,
  they comfort me.

※ *Psalm* 71:21

You will increase my honor
    and comfort me once again.

※ *Psalm* 119:50

My comfort in my suffering is this:
    Your promise preserves my life.

※ *Isaiah* 51:3

The LORD will surely comfort Zion
    and will look with compassion on all her ruins;
he will make her deserts like Eden,
    her wastelands like the garden of the LORD.
Joy and gladness will be found in her,
    thanksgiving and the sound of singing.

※ *Jeremiah* 31:13

Then maidens will dance and be glad,
    young men and old as well.
I will turn their mourning into gladness;
    I will give them comfort and joy instead of sorrow.

✳ 2 Corinthians 1:3–5

Praise be to the God and Father of our Lord Jesus
Christ, the Father of compassion and the God of all
comfort, who comforts us in all our troubles, so that
we can comfort those in any trouble with the comfort
we ourselves have received from God. For just as the
sufferings of Christ flow over into our lives, so also
through Christ our comfort overflows.

compassion

God's Word shows us his concern for people like widows, orphans and the needy. They've had extra pain in life, so God tells us to show them extra compassion. Look around you. Who's hurting in your school or church? A friend whose parents are getting divorced. An acquaintance who just lost a loved one. A girl who sits by herself because she doesn't have any friends. God tells us to seek these people out. Their wounds are raw, and their hearts are needy, so we're to show them extra love. God always looks out for the underdog. Do you?

Stake Your
Life on It!

Does a chipped nail wreck your entire day? If so, it might be time to get your eyes off of yourself and crank up the compassion level! Is your heart broken over what breaks the heart of God?

✳ Micah 7:19

You will again have compassion on us;
* you will tread our sins underfoot*
* and hurl all our iniquities into the depths of the sea.*

✳ Malachi 3:17

"They will be mine," says the LORD Almighty, "in the day when I make up my treasured possession. I will spare them, just as in compassion a man spares his son who serves him."

✳ Matthew 14:14

When Jesus landed and saw a large crowd, he had compassion on them and healed their sick.

✳ Psalm 116:5

The LORD is gracious and righteous;
* our God is full of compassion.*

✳ Psalm 103:13

As a father has compassion on his children,
so the LORD *has compassion on those who fear him.*

✳ 2 Chronicles 30:9

If you return to the LORD, then your brothers and your
children will be shown compassion by their captors and
will come back to this land, for the LORD your God is
gracious and compassionate. He
will not turn his face from you
if you return to him.

❋ Exodus 33:19

And the LORD said, "I will cause all my goodness to pass in front of you, and I will proclaim my name, the LORD, in your presence. I will have mercy on whom I will have mercy, and I will have compassion on whom I will have compassion."

❋ Isaiah 30:18

Yet the LORD longs to be gracious to you;
he rises to show you compassion.
For the LORD is a God of justice.
Blessed are all who wait for him!

❋ Lamentations 3:32

Though he brings grief, he will show compassion,
so great is his unfailing love.

competition

Competition is part of our human nature. In fact, we actually need competition to sharpen our skills. The trouble comes when we constantly compare ourselves to others. Why so? When you compete in athletics, you may win or lose. When you constantly compare yourself to other people, you will always come up short one way or another. Comparison quickly leads to criticism—criticizing others and being critical of yourself. Unchecked competitiveness can quickly get out of control.

Treasured one,
Your world is filled
with so-called "stars"—people who
earn a brief moment of fame for their
achievements or talents or looks.
But true "stars"—those who are wise
in my ways and who guide others
to me—will shine forever!

Your heavenly Father

Ecclesiastes 9:11

I have seen something else under the sun:
The race is not to the swift
    or the battle to the strong,
nor does food come to the wise
    or wealth to the brilliant
    or favor to the learned;
but time and chance happen to them all.

Matthew 19:30

Jesus said, "But many who are first will be last, and many who are last will be first."

Mark 9:35

Sitting down, Jesus called the Twelve and said, "If anyone wants to be first, he must be the very last, and the servant of all."

✳ 1 Corinthians 13:4

Love is patient, love is kind. It does
not envy, it does not boast, it is
not proud.

✳ Philippians 2:3

Do nothing out of selfish ambition or
vain conceit, but in humility consider
others better than yourselves.

✳ Proverbs 24:17

Do not gloat when your enemy falls;
    when he stumbles, do not let your heart rejoice.

✳ 2 Corinthians 10:12

We do not dare to classify or compare ourselves with
some who commend themselves. When they measure
themselves by themselves and compare themselves with
themselves, they are not wise.

1 Corinthians 9:24-25

Do you not know that in a race all the runners run, but only one gets the prize? Run in such a way as to get the prize. Everyone who competes in the games goes into strict training. They do it to get a crown that will not last; but we do it to get a crown that will last forever.

Hebrews 12:1-2

Therefore, since we are surrounded by such a great cloud of witnesses, let us throw off everything that hinders and the sin that so easily entangles, and let us run with perseverance the race marked out for us. Let us fix our eyes on Jesus, the author and perfecter of our faith, who for the joy set before him endured the cross, scorning its shame, and sat down at the right hand of the throne of God.

2 Timothy 2:3-5

Endure hardship with us like a good soldier of Christ Jesus. No one serving as a soldier gets involved in civilian affairs—he wants to please his commanding officer. Similarly, if anyone competes as an athlete, he does not receive the victor's crown unless he competes according to the rules.

contentment

If only I had straight hair . . . if only I were ten pounds thinner . . . if only that guy in English class would notice me. If only. Sometimes our lives are ruled by the "if onlys" and the "what ifs" and the "I wishes." God's Word tells us that true contentment doesn't come from our circumstances. Rather, it is found in Jesus—knowing him, trusting him and depending on his power each day. When you focus on Jesus' priorities and what he wants you to do rather than on what you wish you had, you will find genuine contentment.

Stake Your Life on It!

Let's face it: girls love to shop! But the mall can be a dangerous place when we're struggling to be content. Seeing new stuff often makes us crave what we don't have (and don't really need). Enjoy your shopping, but remember that true contentment isn't about what you have.

✳ *Proverbs 19:23*

The fear of the LORD leads to life:
Then one rests content, untouched by trouble.

✳ *Philippians 4:12–13*

I know what it is to be in need, and I know what it is to
have plenty. I have learned the secret of being content in
any and every situation, whether well fed or hungry,
whether living in plenty or in want. I can do everything
through him who gives me strength.

Psalm 17:14

You still the hunger of those you cherish;
their sons have plenty,
and they store up wealth for their children.

1 Timothy 6:6

But godliness with contentment is great gain.

Psalm 23:1

The LORD is my shepherd, I shall not be in want.

Proverbs 30:15–16

The leech has two daughters.
   "Give! Give!" they cry.
There are three things that are never satisfied,
   four that never say, "Enough!":
the grave, the barren womb,
   land, which is never satisfied with water,
   and fire, which never says, "Enough!"

Ecclesiastes 5:19

Moreover, when God gives any man wealth and
possessions, and enables him to enjoy them, to accept his
lot and be happy in his work—this is a gift of God.

courage

On a scale of 1 to 10 (with 10 being "completely courageous" and 1 being "a wimp"), how courageous are you? In the Old Testament, Queen Esther risked her life to go before the king and speak on behalf of her people. That's about a 12 on a 10-point courage scale! You may not have to risk your life to prove your courage. But you might have to do something outside of your comfort zone—like speaking to your friends about God or not giving in to peer pressure even though everyone else is. Are you courageous enough to do what it takes?

Stake Your Life on It!

It's scary to serve God when you don't fully understand his plan, especially when others might make fun of you. Be brave. Take a stand and trust in God.

✳ Isaiah 41:10

So do not fear, for I am with you;
*   do not be dismayed, for I am your God.*
I will strengthen you and help you;
*   I will uphold you with my righteous right hand.*

✳ Isaiah 35:4

Say to those with fearful hearts,
*   "Be strong, do not fear;*
your God will come,
*   he will come with vengeance;*
with divine retribution
*   he will come to save you."*

✳ Lamentations 3:57

You came near when I called you,
*   and you said, "Do not fear."*

✳ Acts 4:13

When they saw the courage of Peter and John and
realized that they were unschooled, ordinary men, they
were astonished and they took note that these men had
been with Jesus.

✳ Philippians 1:20

I eagerly expect and hope that I will in no way be
ashamed, but will have sufficient courage so that now as
always Christ will be exalted in my body, whether by life
or by death.

✳ 1 Corinthians 16:13

Be on your guard; stand firm in the faith;
be men of courage; be strong.

✳ Deuteronomy 31:6

Be strong and courageous. Do not be afraid or terrified
because of them, for the LORD your God goes with you;
he will never leave you nor forsake you.

* Psalm 118:6

The LORD is with me; I will not be afraid.
What can man do to me?

* Matthew 10:28

Jesus said, "Do not be afraid of those
who kill the body but cannot kill the
soul. Rather, be afraid of the One
who can destroy both soul and
body in hell."

Remember the romance of Samson and Delilah? Obviously, Samson wasn't using his head. He thought he was in love with Delilah, so nothing else mattered to him. He wasn't the first one to fall into this trap—and he certainly wasn't the last. It's a common story for us girls: A girl thinks she's in love with a guy, and so she does a lot of things she never thought she'd do—like changing her personality to fit his, dropping her friends to be with him or going farther sexually because he pushed her to. Don't let that be you! In your relationships, make sure your head has control over your heart.

Stake Your
Life on It!

While you may dream about getting married someday, did you know you're already a bride? The church (all faithful believers) is Jesus' bride. Be pure and spotless for him.

✳ Proverbs 4:23

Above all else, guard your heart,
*   for it is the wellspring of life.*

✳ 1 Thessalonians 4:3–5

It is God's will that you should be sanctified: that you should avoid sexual immorality; that each of you should learn to control his own body in a way that is holy and honorable, not in passionate lust like the heathen, who do not know God.

✳ *Hebrews* 13:4

Marriage should be honored by all, and the
marriage bed kept pure, for God will judge
the adulterer and all the sexually immoral.

✳ 2 *Corinthians* 6:14

Do not be yoked together with
unbelievers. For what do righteousness
and wickedness have in common?
Or what fellowship can light have
with darkness?

✳ Colossians 3:12

Therefore, as God's chosen people, holy and dearly loved, clothe yourselves with compassion, kindness, humility, gentleness and patience.

depression

Are you feelin' down? Discouraged about life? Wondering if maybe you'll never really amount to much of anything, never really matter, never really make a difference? Wondering if doing the right thing is worth all the effort? When you're feeling depressed, there are lots of ways you can search for encouragement: seeking out friends, distracting yourself with music or movies, losing yourself in sports or school or work. But those things can't compare with what you'll find in God. He's the source of "eternal encouragement and good hope" (2 Thessalonians 2:16). When you're having a low day, look to him for new strength.

Dear daughter,

When you are hurting, come to me. When you are lonely or depressed, seek me. When your struggles threaten to overwhelm you, there is only one solution: Seek me and live! I alone am the answer to your problems.

Father God

✳ Lamentations 3:19–26

I remember my affliction and my wandering,
the bitterness and the gall.
I well remember them,
and my soul is downcast within me.
Yet this I call to mind
and therefore I have hope:

Because of the LORD's great love we are not consumed,
for his compassions never fail.
They are new every morning;
great is your faithfulness.
I say to myself, "The LORD is my portion;
therefore I will wait for him."

The LORD is good to those whose hope is in him,
to the one who seeks him;
it is good to wait quietly
for the salvation of the LORD.

* 2 Corinthians 1:9–10

Indeed, in our hearts we felt the sentence of death. But this happened that we might not rely on ourselves but on God, who raises the dead. He has delivered us from such a deadly peril, and he will deliver us. On him we have set our hope that he will continue to deliver us.

* Psalm 71:20

Though you have made me see troubles, many and bitter,
  you will restore my life again;
from the depths of the earth
  you will again bring me up.

Psalm 30:5

For his anger lasts only a moment,
but his favor lasts a lifetime;
weeping may remain for a night,
but rejoicing comes in the morning.

John 16:33

I have told you these things, so that in me you may have peace. In this world you will have trouble. But take heart! I have overcome the world.

emotions

There's nothing like a good cry. Sometimes we need to just let our emotions out, you know? Maybe you can identify with the psalms David wrote. He flooded his bed with weeping and drenched his couch with tears. And God's fine with that. He wants you to bring him your fears, sorrows, hurts and tears. Like David, you'll find that God hears your weeping and accepts your prayer. Be honest with God, even through your tears. He already knows how you feel, and he wants to comfort you. So go ahead and cry! Then let God wipe away the tears.

Stake Your
Life on It!

Emotions aren't bad. They're part of God's design. Figuring out how to control them is the key. Proverbs 17:27 describes a person with emotional maturity as being even-tempered. Now that's not going to happen overnight, but you can work on it.

❋ Hebrews 4:12

For the word of God is living and active. Sharper than any double-edged sword, it penetrates even to dividing soul and spirit, joints and marrow; it judges the thoughts and attitudes of the heart.

❋ 1 Peter 5:7

Cast all your anxiety on him because he cares for you.

Philippians 4:4-7

Rejoice in the Lord always. I will say it again: Rejoice!
Let your gentleness be evident to all. The Lord is near.
Do not be anxious about anything, but in everything,
by prayer and petition, with thanksgiving, present your
requests to God. And the peace of God, which transcends
all understanding, will guard your hearts and your minds
in Christ Jesus.

1 John 4:18

There is no fear in love. But perfect love drives out fear,
because fear has to do with punishment. The one who
fears is not made perfect in love.

❉ **Matthew 5:4**

Jesus said, "Blessed are those who mourn,
   for they will be comforted."

❉ **Isaiah 32:17**

The fruit of righteousness will be peace;
   the effect of righteousness will be quietness
      and confidence forever.

failure

Which is harder: (1) to fail, or (2) to keep going after you've failed? Number 2, right? Anyone can fail at something. But to keep going—to persevere—is one challenge many of us, well, fail to do. Solomon, the wisest king in the world, sinned by marrying foreign women who led him into worshiping idols. Whoops. Whether he returned to God after that is anyone's guess. Faith takes perseverance. Even if you fail—a month without devotions, a season of prayerlessness, giving in to peer pressure—you have to get back on your feet and keep going. Genuine faith never quits.

Dear loved one,

There may be times when you will fail me.

There may be times when I am disappointed with your

choices or actions. But I will never turn my back

on you or exclude you from my presence.

Everlasting Father

* *Psalm 71:20*

Though you have made me see troubles, many and bitter,
   you will restore my life again;
from the depths of the earth
   you will again bring me up.

* *Psalm 73:26*

My flesh and my heart may fail,
   but God is the strength of my heart
   and my portion forever.

✳ 2 Corinthians 12:9

But he said to me, "My grace is sufficient for you, for my power is made perfect in weakness." Therefore I will boast all the more gladly about my weaknesses, so that Christ's power may rest on me.

✳ 1 Corinthians 1:26–29

Brothers, think of what you were when you were called. Not many of you were wise by human standards; not many were influential; not many were of noble birth. But God chose the foolish things of the world to shame the wise; God chose the weak things of the world to shame the strong. He chose the lowly things of this world and the despised things—and the things that are not—to nullify the things that are, so that no one may boast before him.

✳ Romans 8:33–34

Who will bring any charge against those whom God has chosen? It is God who justifies. Who is he that condemns? Christ Jesus, who died—more than that, who was raised to life—is at the right hand of God and is also interceding for us.

Romans 8:26

In the same way, the Spirit helps us in our weakness. We do not know what we ought to pray for, but the Spirit himself intercedes for us with groans that words cannot express.

2 Corinthians 4:7–11

But we have this treasure in jars of clay to show that this all-surpassing power is from God and not from us. We are hard pressed on every side, but not crushed; perplexed, but not in despair; persecuted, but not abandoned; struck down, but not destroyed. We always carry around in our body the death of Jesus, so that the life of Jesus may also be revealed in our body. For we who are alive are always being given over to death for Jesus' sake, so that his life may be revealed in our mortal body.

Luke 13:30

Jesus said, "Indeed there are those who are last who will be first, and first who will be last."

faith

Nothing is too hard for God. You hear that?! No thing. God made the heavens and the earth, and he can do anything! Turning the most hardened, rebellious jerk you know into a kind, generous follower of Jesus—that's easy. Fixing your broken relationships with your parents or your friends—no big deal. Helping you make sense out of the crazy, mixed-up madness you call your life— definitely a piece of cake. Nothing is too hard for God. Have faith that he can do all things.

Stake Your
Life on It!

Want success in prayer, ministry or life? You've got to have faith. You don't have to be the model of perfection in order to see God's power—you just need that mustard seed of pure faith.

❋ Hebrews 11:1

Now faith is being sure of what we hope for and certain of what we do not see.

❋ Hebrews 11:6

And without faith it is impossible to please God, because anyone who comes to him must believe that he exists and that he rewards those who earnestly seek him.

❋ James 2:17

In the same way, faith by itself, if it is not accompanied by action, is dead.

*Luke 7:50

Jesus said to the woman, "Your faith has saved you; go in peace."

*Romans 3:22

This righteousness from God comes through faith in Jesus Christ to all who believe. There is no difference.

*Romans 5:1

Therefore, since we have been justified through faith, we have peace with God through our Lord Jesus Christ.

*Ephesians 3:12

In him and through faith in him we may approach God with freedom and confidence.

*2 Corinthians 5:7

We live by faith, not by sight.

※ **Matthew** 21:21

Jesus said, "I tell you the truth, if you have faith and do not doubt, not only can you do what was done to the fig tree, but also you can say to this mountain, 'Go, throw yourself into the sea,' and it will be done."

※ **James** 5:15

And the prayer offered in faith will make the sick person well; the Lord will raise him up. If he has sinned, he will be forgiven.

※ **1 John** 5:4

For everyone born of God overcomes the world. This is the victory that has overcome the world, even our faith.

Finals are coming up, you need to memorize lines for the play, and you have extra practices before basketball playoffs. Your parents expect you to keep up with chores, babysit your little sister and be there for "family time." You can barely juggle all your own commitments, let alone help out anybody else! You think you've got a lot going on— check out Jesus. On the cross, Jesus looked beyond his own pain and his own issues to make sure that his mom was taken care of (John 19:25–27). Let's just say it's a matter of priorities sometimes.

❋ *Psalm 68:6*

God sets the lonely in families,
*   he leads forth the prisoners with singing;*
*   but the rebellious live in a sun-scorched land.*

❋ *John 8:35*

Jesus said, "Now a slave has no permanent place in the family, but a son belongs to it forever."

Stake Your Life on It!

Are you stuck with some family baggage—divorce, drug or alcohol addiction, cruddy relationships, abuse? No matter how bleak the situation looks, don't give up on your family. There is no pain beyond God's healing, no problem too great for his power. Keep praying!

* Proverbs 11:29

He who brings trouble on his family will inherit only wind,
and the fool will be servant to the wise.

* 1 Timothy 3:5

If anyone does not know how to manage his own family,
how can he take care of God's church?

* 1 Timothy 5:4

But if a widow has children or grandchildren, these
should learn first of all to put their religion into practice
by caring for their own family and so repaying their
parents and grandparents, for this is pleasing to God.

* Deuteronomy 5:16

Honor your father and your mother, as the LORD your
God has commanded you, so that you may live long and
that it may go well with you in the land the LORD your
God is giving you.

Mark 5:19

Jesus said, "Go home to your family and tell them how much the Lord has done for you, and how he has had mercy on you."

2 Timothy 1:5

I have been reminded of your sincere faith, which first lived in your grandmother Lois and in your mother Eunice and, I am persuaded, now lives in you also.

Hebrews 2:11

Both the one who makes men holy and those who are made holy are of the same family. So Jesus is not ashamed to call them brothers.

forgiveness

Imagine spilling an entire bottle of fire-engine-red nail polish all over your new white sweater. Talk about disaster! No matter how hard you try to wash it out, it's unlikely your sweater will ever be completely white again. Sin is like that bright red polish, and it has left you with a permanent stain that you can't get rid of. But God can. He is able to take your sin, no matter how bad it is, and remove it completely. He can make you white as snow. Confess your sin to him, and be confident that you will be made perfectly clean.

Daughter,

It doesn't matter how far you wander

from me in this world, what detours you take,

how many mistakes you make or how badly you mess up.

When you return, I run to you with open arms,

ready to welcome you home.

Your Father

*Isaiah 1:18

"Come now, let us reason together,"
  says the LORD.
"Though your sins are like scarlet,
  they shall be as white as snow;
though they are red as crimson,
  they shall be like wool."

*1 John 1:9

If we confess our sins, he is faithful and just and will
forgive us our sins and purify us from all
unrighteousness.

*Matthew 26:27–28

Then Jesus took the cup, gave thanks and offered it to
them, saying, "Drink from it, all of you. This is my
blood of the covenant, which is poured out for many for
the forgiveness of sins."

*Acts 13:38

Therefore, my brothers, I want you to know that through Jesus the forgiveness of sins is proclaimed to you.

*Acts 5:31

God exalted him to his own right hand as Prince and Savior that he might give repentance and forgiveness of sins to Israel.

*Ephesians 1:7

In him we have redemption through his blood, the forgiveness of sins, in accordance with the riches of God's grace.

*2 Chronicles 7:14

If my people, who are called by my name, will humble themselves and pray and seek my face and turn from their wicked ways, then will I hear from heaven and will forgive their sin and will heal their land.

*Jeremiah 33:8

I will cleanse them from all the sin they have committed against me and will forgive all their sins of rebellion against me.

Psalm 130:4

But with you there is forgiveness;
 therefore you are feared.

Matthew 6:14–15

Jesus said, "For if you forgive men when they sin against
you, your heavenly Father will also forgive you. But if
you do not forgive men their sins, your Father will not
forgive your sins."

Luke 17:3–4

Jesus said, "So watch yourselves. If your brother sins,
rebuke him, and if he repents, forgive him. If he sins
against you seven times in a day, and seven times comes
back to you and says, 'I repent,' forgive him."

Colossians 3:13

Bear with each other and forgive whatever grievances
you may have against one another. Forgive as the Lord
forgave you.

friendship

Your true friends are those you can count on even when you feel moody, even when you're not at your best, even when you're going through an ugly stage, even when you don't make the team or get the award. A true friend loves at all times. Some girls will only be "friends" with you if they think that your friendship will somehow help them. But friendship is about being there through the good times and the bad, and that's usually when you need your friends the most! What kind of friend are you?

Stake Your
Life on It!

All friendships go through tense times. It's natural! Sometimes the best way to keep a friendship tight is to just give each other a little space.

* **Proverbs 12:26**

A righteous man is cautious in friendship,
  but the way of the wicked leads them astray.

* **James 4:4**

You adulterous people, don't you know that friendship with the world is hatred toward God? Anyone who chooses to be a friend of the world becomes an enemy of God.

* **Ecclesiastes 4:10–12**

If one falls down,
  his friend can help him up.
But pity the man who falls
  and has no one to help him up!
Also, if two lie down together, they will keep warm.
  But how can one keep warm alone?
Though one may be overpowered,
  two can defend themselves.
A cord of three strands is not quickly broken.

＊ Psalm 119:63

I am a friend to all who fear you,
    to all who follow your precepts.

＊ Proverbs 18:24

A man of many companions may come to ruin,
    but there is a friend who sticks closer than a brother.

Proverbs 27:6

Wounds from a friend can be trusted,
but an enemy multiplies kisses.

John 15:13–15

Jesus said, "Greater love has no one than this, that he lay
down his life for his friends. You are my friends if you do
what I command. I no longer call you servants, because a
servant does not know his master's business. Instead,
I have called you friends, for everything that I learned
from my Father I have made known to you."

1 John 4:7

Dear friends, let us love one another, for love comes
from God. Everyone who loves has been born of God
and knows God.

future

When you think about your future—picking a college, pursuing a career, maybe getting married and starting a family—do you ever wonder what life is all about? What's the purpose? It seems like such a big, complicated question. But the answer is very simple: God created you for his glory. That's it. That's all there is to it. And you will find the truest joy and peace and satisfaction in life when you fulfill that purpose. As you make decisions about your future, remember that you were created to bring God glory—that's what it's all about.

My child,

The uncertainties of the future can fill you with fear.

But you can face your eternal future

with confidence. You have your own room in my Father's

house. I know this because I prepared it for you myself.

And I will return to take you there.

Lord Jesus

* **Jeremiah 29:11**

"For I know the plans I have for you," declares the
LORD, "plans to prosper you and not to harm you,
plans to give you hope and a future."

* **Isaiah 14:24**

The LORD Almighty has sworn,
"Surely, as I have planned, so it will be,
    and as I have purposed, so it will stand."

* **Romans 8:38–39**

For I am convinced that neither death nor life, neither
angels nor demons, neither the present nor the future,
nor any powers, neither height nor depth, nor anything
else in all creation, will be able to separate us from the
love of God that is in Christ Jesus our Lord.

✳ **Psalm 37:37**

Consider the blameless, observe the upright;
*   there is a future for the man of peace.*

✳ **Proverbs 24:14**

Know also that wisdom is sweet to your soul;
*   if you find it, there is a future hope for you,*
*   and your hope will not be cut off.*

✳ **Ecclesiastes 7:14**

When times are good, be happy;
*   but when times are bad, consider:*
God has made the one
*   as well as the other.*
Therefore, a man cannot discover
*   anything about his future.*

✳ Matthew 6:34

Jesus said, "Therefore do not worry about tomorrow, for tomorrow will worry about itself. Each day has enough trouble of its own."

✳ Proverbs 27:1

Do not boast about tomorrow,
    for you do not know what a day may bring forth.

✳ James 4:13–15

Now listen, you who say, "Today or tomorrow we will go to this or that city, spend a year there, carry on business and make money." Why, you do not even know what will happen tomorrow. What is your life? You are a mist that appears for a little while and then vanishes. Instead, you ought to say, "If it is the Lord's will, we will live and do this or that."

happiness

God wants you to be a party girl. What?! That can't be! But it's true. God wants you to be happy and enjoy life, each and every day he's given you. Ultimately, he wants you to find your joy in him. You see, all the good things that you experience come from his hand, and he intends for you to enjoy them as gifts from him. He wants you to celebrate the life that he has given you and to find your happiness in him.

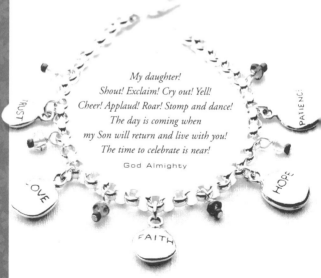

My daughter!
Shout! Exclaim! Cry out! Yell!
Cheer! Applaud! Roar! Stomp and dance!
The day is coming when
my Son will return and live with you!
The time to celebrate is near!

God Almighty

Psalm 16:11

You have made known to me the path of life;
  you will fill me with joy in your presence,
  with eternal pleasures at your right hand.

Psalm 30:11

You turned my wailing into dancing;
  you removed my sackcloth and clothed me with joy,

Isaiah 12:3

With joy you will draw water
  from the wells of salvation.

Ecclesiastes 8:15

So I commend the enjoyment of life, because nothing is better for a man under the sun than to eat and drink and be glad. Then joy will accompany him in his work all the days of the life God has given him under the sun.

Ecclesiastes 5:19

Moreover, when God gives any man wealth and possessions, and enables him to enjoy them, to accept his lot and be happy in his work—this is a gift of God.

James 5:13

Is anyone happy? Let him sing songs of praise.

Psalm 68:3

*But may the righteous be glad
    and rejoice before God;
    may they be happy and joyful.*

✳ Isaiah 51:11

The ransomed of the LORD will return.
*   They will enter Zion with singing;*
*   everlasting joy will crown their heads.*
Gladness and joy will overtake them,
*   and sorrow and sighing will flee away.*

✳ Zechariah 2:10

"Shout and be glad, O Daughter of Zion. For I am
coming, and I will live among you," declares the LORD.

✳ Revelation 19:7

Let us rejoice and be glad
*   and give him glory!*
For the wedding of the Lamb has come,
*   and his bride has made herself ready.*

hope

When you're in a tight spot, it's tough to wait for God to respond and save you. The best way to keep up your hope through a tough time is to remember what God has done for you in the past. Remembering all that God did for you in past crises can give you hope that he'll come through for you again. Preach it to yourself, sista! Remind yourself that even when you can't see God, he's at work. Even when you can't feel God, he's by your side. Even when you're unstable, he's constant. Hope is a powerful thing.

Stake Your Life on It!

Do you sometimes feel like you're a little boat, drifting all alone on the sea of life? What you need is an anchor! And there's only one that's strong enough and secure enough to hold you. Place your faith in Christ, and you'll discover you have a hope that will anchor your soul— no matter how stormy life gets.

* **Psalm 25:3**

No one whose hope is in you
*   will ever be put to shame,*
but they will be put to shame
*   who are treacherous without excuse.*

* **Psalm 33:17–18**

A horse is a vain hope for deliverance;
*   despite all its great strength it cannot save.*
But the eyes of the LORD are on those who fear him,
*   on those whose hope is in his unfailing love.*

* **Proverbs 23:18**

There is surely a future hope for you,
*   and your hope will not be cut off.*

* **Isaiah 40:31**

But those who hope in the LORD
*   will renew their strength.*
They will soar on wings like eagles;
*   they will run and not grow weary,*
*   they will walk and not be faint.*

✳ Romans 5:5

And hope does not disappoint us, because God has poured out his love into our hearts by the Holy Spirit, whom he has given us.

✳ Romans 8:24–25

For in this hope we were saved. But hope that is seen is no hope at all. Who hopes for what he already has? But if we hope for what we do not yet have, we wait for it patiently.

✳ Romans 15:4

For everything that was written in the past was written to teach us, so that through endurance and the encouragement of the Scriptures we might have hope.

✳ 2 Corinthians 3:12

Therefore, since we have such a hope, we are very bold.

1 Timothy 6:17

Command those who are rich in
this present world not to be
arrogant nor to put their hope
in wealth, which is so uncertain,
but to put their hope in God,
who richly provides us with
everything for our enjoyment.

Hebrews 10:23

Let us hold unswervingly to the
hope we profess, for he who promised
is faithful.

1 Peter 3:15

But in your hearts set apart Christ as
Lord. Always be prepared to give an
answer to everyone who asks you to give
the reason for the hope that you have.

1 John 3:3

Everyone who has this hope in him purifies
himself, just as he is pure.

identity

It can be painful to compare yourself to other girls. Some girls are prettier, some have cooler clothes, some are more athletic, some get better grades, some get all the guys. Of course, those girls are also looking around and seeing other girls who are prettier, more athletic, smarter and more popular. The truth is, there's always someone better than you at something. Your true identity doesn't depend on how you compare to others. Remember that you are "wonderfully made" by God—and God doesn't make mistakes (Psalm 139:14). You are valuable because you are his!

Loved one,

This time of your life can feel confusing—

about what you want and feel, even about who you are.

Focus on me. I understand you perfectly and

will help you learn more about yourself.

The One who understands you

✳ Genesis 1:27

So God created man in his own image,
*   in the image of God he created him;*
*   male and female he created them.*

✳ Psalm 139:13–16

For you created my inmost being;
*   you knit me together in my mother's womb.*
I praise you because I am fearfully and wonderfully made;
*   your works are wonderful,*
*   I know that full well.*
My frame was not hidden from you
*   when I was made in the secret place.*
When I was woven together in the depths of the earth,
*   your eyes saw my unformed body.*
All the days ordained for me
*   were written in your book*
*   before one of them came to be.*

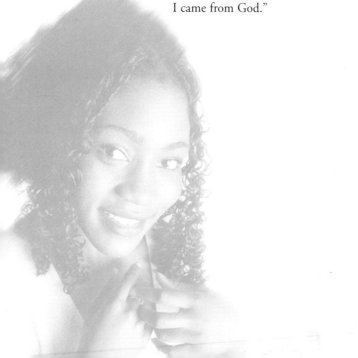

✴ *Luke* 12:7

Jesus said, "Indeed, the very hairs of your head are all numbered. Don't be afraid; you are worth more than many sparrows."

✴ *John* 16:27

Jesus said, "The Father himself loves you because you have loved me and have believed that I came from God."

Ephesians 2:10

For we are God's workmanship, created in Christ Jesus to do good works, which God prepared in advance for us to do.

2 Corinthians 5:17

Therefore, if anyone is in Christ, he is a new creation; the old has gone, the new has come!

1 Corinthians 12:7–11

Now to each one the manifestation of the Spirit is given for the common good. To one there is given through the Spirit the message of wisdom, to another the message of knowledge by means of the same Spirit, to another faith by the same Spirit, to another gifts of healing by that one Spirit, to another miraculous powers, to another prophecy, to another distinguishing between spirits, to another speaking in different kinds of tongues, and to still another the interpretation of tongues. All these are the work of one and the same Spirit, and he gives them to each one, just as he determines.

integrity

How do you act when things aren't going your way? Does your personality change (hello, temper tantrum!), or do you act the same way regardless? When you have integrity, you do the right thing, even when you don't feel like it. We can learn a lot about integrity from the Old Testament character Job. After their children died and they lost just about everything, Job and his wife responded with two extremes. Job's wife advised him to curse God. But Job held on to his integrity and kept consistent, godly character even when life got hard. Which one are you more like—Job or his wife?

Stake Your Life on It!

Isn't it crazy how you can know what's right but keep doing what's wrong?! As long as we're alive we'll struggle with sin. Thank God that Jesus rescues us!

✳ **Psalm 41:12**

In my integrity you uphold me
and set me in your presence forever.

✳ **Proverbs 10:9**

The man of integrity walks securely,
but he who takes crooked paths will be found out.

✳ **Proverbs 11:3**

The integrity of the upright guides them,
but the unfaithful are destroyed by their duplicity.

✳ **Romans 1:17**

For in the gospel a righteousness from God is revealed, a righteousness that is by faith from first to last, just as it is written: "The righteous will live by faith."

✳ 2 Corinthians 5:21

God made him who had no sin to be sin for us, so that in him we might become the righteousness of God.

✳ Galatians 5:5

But by faith we eagerly await through the Spirit the righteousness for which we hope.

✳ Isaiah 26:7

The path of the righteous is level;
    O upright One, you make the way of the righteous smooth.

* Deuteronomy 32:4

He is the Rock, his works are perfect,
*   and all his ways are just.*
A faithful God who does no wrong,
*   upright and just is he.*

* Psalm 11:7

For the LORD is righteous,
*   he loves justice;*
*   upright men will see his face.*

loneliness

Do you know what it feels like to be excluded? To be the outsider, the one girl sitting alone, hoping to be invited in? God tells us to treat girls on the fringe with extra compassion. We all go through seasons of loneliness. And there are no easy answers or quick solutions. Remember, though, that you're never truly alone. God longs to comfort you whenever you feel alone or rejected.

Stake Your
Life on It!

If you're feeling like the odd girl out, remember, you're not the only one who feels alone and needs a friend. Find another girl who's lonely and make an effort to befriend her. Focusing on someone else's need helps lessen your own pain.

* Genesis 2:18

The LORD God said, "It is not good for the man to be alone. I will make a helper suitable for him."

* Psalm 102:7,12–13

I lie awake; I have become
  like a bird alone on a roof . . . .
But you, O LORD, sit enthroned forever;
  your renown endures through all generations.
You will arise and have compassion on Zion,
  for it is time to show favor to her;
  the appointed time has come.

* John 15:15

Jesus said, "I no longer call you servants, because a servant does not know his master's business. Instead, I have called you friends, for everything that I learned from my Father I have made known to you."

✷ *Ephesians* 2:19–21

Consequently, you are no longer foreigners and aliens, but fellow citizens with God's people and members of God's household, built on the foundation of the apostles and prophets, with Christ Jesus himself as the chief cornerstone. In him the whole building is joined together and rises to become a holy temple in the Lord.

✷ 2 *Timothy* 4:16–17

At my first defense, no one came to my support, but everyone deserted me. May it not be held against them. But the Lord stood at my side and gave me strength, so that through me the message might be fully proclaimed and all the Gentiles might hear it. And I was delivered from the lion's mouth.

Romans 8:38-39

For I am convinced that neither death nor life, neither angels nor demons, neither the present nor the future, nor any powers, neither height nor depth, nor anything else in all creation, will be able to separate us from the love of God that is in Christ Jesus our Lord.

Isaiah 49:14-15

But Zion said, "The LORD has forsaken me,
the Lord has forgotten me."
Can a mother forget the baby at her breast
and have no compassion on the child she has borne?
Though she may forget,
I will not forget you!

loving God

To what could your love for (or faithfulness to) God be compared? Something permanent like ink stains? Semi-permanent like a marker? Something that quickly fades like a light pencil mark? Would God agree with you? During the Old Testament prophet Hosea's day, God compared the love of the people of Israel to the morning mist. In other words, it was temporary. Ouch. They weren't very faithful to God! This was obvious in their lack of sorrow over their sin. How deep is your love? If your love is "leaded" (get it—pencil lead?), why not ask the Lord to make it deeper and richer?

Stake Your Life on It!

God doesn't want to share you with other loves and desires. He only fits into a life that has been offered to him fully. What other loves are you still holding on to?

* 1 John 4:9–10

This is how God showed his love among us: He sent his one and only Son into the world that we might live through him. This is love: not that we loved God, but that he loved us and sent his Son as an atoning sacrifice for our sins.

* John 3:16

Jesus said, "For God so loved the world that he gave his one and only Son, that whoever believes in him shall not perish but have eternal life."

* Ephesians 3:17–19

So that Christ may dwell in your hearts through faith. And I pray that you, being rooted and established in love, may have power, together with all the saints, to grasp how wide and long and high and deep is the love of Christ, and to know this love that surpasses knowledge— that you may be filled to the measure of all the fullness of God.

Ephesians 2:4–5

But because of his great love for us, God, who is rich in mercy, made us alive with Christ even when we were dead in transgressions—it is by grace you have been saved.

1 John 3:1

How great is the love the Father has lavished on us, that we should be called children of God! And that is what we are! The reason the world does not know us is that it did not know him.

Lamentations 3:22

Because of the LORD's great love we are not consumed,
*   for his compassions never fail.*

Jeremiah 31:3

The LORD appeared to us in the past, saying:
*   "I have loved you with an everlasting love;*
*   I have drawn you with loving-kindness."*

Psalm 36:5

Your love, O LORD, reaches to the heavens,
*   your faithfulness to the skies.*

Psalm 63:3

Because your love is better than life,
*   my lips will glorify you.*

loving others

Have you ever seen what happens when you shake a can of soda really, really hard, then open it up fast? The soda sprays out all over the person holding the can and probably even covers the people nearby, too. Did you know God wants you to be like that can? God wants your life to be so full of love that it overflows and spills out onto everyone around you. God has poured his love into you so that you can share it with others. So go ahead—shake it up and spray it out!

Stake Your Life on It!

Since God loves everyone, what does it say about your love for him when you totally dismiss someone he sent his Son to die for? We show our love for God by loving others.

* John 13:34–35

Jesus said, "A new command I give you: Love one another. As I have loved you, so you must love one another. By this all men will know that you are my disciples, if you love one another."

* 1 Corinthians 13:4–7

Love is patient, love is kind. It does not envy, it does not boast, it is not proud. It is not rude, it is not self-seeking, it is not easily angered, it keeps no record of wrongs. Love does not delight in evil but rejoices with the truth. It always protects, always trusts, always hopes, always perseveres.

1 John 4:8

Whoever does not love does not know God, because God is love.

1 John 4:12

No one has ever seen God; but if we love one another, God lives in us and his love is made complete in us.

✳ Romans 13:8

Let no debt remain outstanding, except the continuing debt to love one another, for he who loves his fellowman has fulfilled the law.

✳ Colossians 3:14

And over all these virtues put on love, which binds them all together in perfect unity.

✳ 1 Peter 4:8

Above all, love each other deeply, because love covers over a multitude of sins.

✳ 1 Peter 1:22

Now that you have purified yourselves by obeying the truth so that you have sincere love for your brothers, love one another deeply, from the heart.

materialism

What is your most prized possession? The diamond earrings that were your grandmother's? That top-of-the-line pocket PC with the built-in cell phone? The black leather jacket you bought with your own money? No matter how great that thing is, it's not going to last forever. Diamonds get stolen, PC's become obsolete, and leather gets worn and goes out of style. That's why it's important to value the things you can't see—like love and obedience to God—because they do last forever. Invest your time, money and energy into those things, and you'll find yourself with everlasting treasure.

Stake Your Life on It!

It's so easy to be defined by your possessions, isn't it? But your life is meant to be about so much more than your stuff. Make sure that, above all else, you have a rich relationship with God. That's all that really counts.

* Matthew 6:33

Jesus said, "But seek first his kingdom and his righteousness, and all these things will be given to you as well."

* Luke 12:33-34

Jesus said, "Sell your possessions and give to the poor. Provide purses for yourselves that will not wear out, a treasure in heaven that will not be exhausted, where no thief comes near and no moth destroys. For where your treasure is, there your heart will be also."

✳ Ecclesiastes 5:10

Whoever loves money never has money enough;
    whoever loves wealth is never satisfied with his income.
    This too is meaningless.

✳ Isaiah 55:2

Why spend money on what is not bread,
    and your labor on what does not satisfy?
Listen, listen to me, and eat what is good,
    and your soul will delight in the richest of fare.

✳ Proverbs 17:16

Of what use is money in the hand of a fool,
    since he has no desire to get wisdom?

✳ Matthew 6:24

Jesus said, "No one can serve two masters. Either he will hate the one and love the other, or he will be devoted to the one and despise the other. You cannot serve both God and Money."

Acts 8:20

Peter answered: "May your money perish with you, because you thought you could buy the gift of God with money!"

1 Timothy 6:10

For the love of money is a root of all kinds of evil. Some people, eager for money, have wandered from the faith and pierced themselves with many griefs.

Hebrews 13:5

Keep your lives free from the love of money and be content with what you have, because God has said,
"Never will I leave you;
    never will I forsake you."

obedience

Obeying God is not like extra credit on a test—as in nice but not necessary. It's the whole test, and you either pass or you fail. Sometimes God asks us to do things that we don't understand. It's tempting to ask why or to wonder how it's going to end. But God doesn't tell us the whole story up front. He wants us to make the tough choices and then to trust him. Do you always speak truth—even when a "little white lie" would make life so much easier? Do you steer clear of gossip—even when there's "juicy news" just begging to be shared? God doesn't consider any of his commands to be optional. Neither should you.

Stake Your
Life on It!

When God set the rules for life, he didn't create an impossible dream. You don't even have to be a Bible scholar. The Christian life is well within your reach.

✳ Exodus 19:5-6

Now if you obey me fully and keep my covenant, then out of all nations you will be my treasured possession. Although the whole earth is mine, you will be for me a kingdom of priests and a holy nation.

✳ Leviticus 25:18

Follow my decrees and be careful to obey my laws, and you will live safely in the land.

✳ Deuteronomy 30:12-14

It is not up in heaven, so that you have to ask, "Who will ascend into heaven to get it and proclaim it to us so we may obey it?" Nor is it beyond the sea, so that you have to ask, "Who will cross the sea to get it and proclaim it to us so we may obey it?" No, the word is very near you; it is in your mouth and in your heart so you may obey it.

* **1 Samuel 15:22**

But Samuel replied:
"Does the LORD delight in burnt offerings and sacrifices
 as much as in obeying the voice of the LORD?
To obey is better than sacrifice,
 and to heed is better than the fat of rams."

* **Psalm 119:100**

I have more understanding than the elders,
 for I obey your precepts.

* **Luke 11:28**

Jesus said, "Blessed rather are those who hear the word of
God and obey it."

* **John 14:23**

Jesus said, "If anyone loves me, he will obey my
teaching. My Father will love him, and we will come to
him and make our home with him."

Romans 5:19

For just as through the disobedience of the one man the many were made sinners, so also through the obedience of the one man the many will be made righteous.

Romans 6:16

Don't you know that when you offer yourselves to someone to obey him as slaves, you are slaves to the one whom you obey—whether you are slaves to sin, which leads to death, or to obedience, which leads to righteousness?

1 John 5:3

This is love for God: to obey his commands. And his commands are not burdensome.

peer pressure

Have you ever done something you shouldn't have done because you were afraid? Maybe you smoked or drank because you were scared your friends would think less of you if you didn't. Maybe you slept with your boyfriend because you were afraid of losing him to another girl. Maybe you let a guy cheat off your test because you were afraid he'd make fun of you if you didn't. Don't ever let fear of what other people might think or do overshadow doing what God wants you to do. He is the only one we are to fear, revere and trust. He's stronger and more important than any person.

Loved one,

When others are pulling you in different directions,

urging you to come and follow them,

remember my promise. I will give you an undivided heart,

a focus and purpose that will not lead you astray.

Your loving Father

* Romans 12:1-2

Therefore, I urge you, brothers, in view of God's mercy, to offer your bodies as living sacrifices, holy and pleasing to God—this is your spiritual act of worship. Do not conform any longer to the pattern of this world, but be transformed by the renewing of your mind. Then you will be able to test and approve what God's will is— his good, pleasing and perfect will.

* 1 John 2:15-17

Do not love the world or anything in the world. If anyone loves the world, the love of the Father is not in him. For everything in the world—the cravings of sinful man, the lust of his eyes and the boasting of what he has and does—comes not from the Father but from the world. The world and its desires pass away, but the man who does the will of God lives forever.

1 Corinthians 15:33

Do not be misled: "Bad company corrupts good character."

Proverbs 1:10

My son, if sinners entice you,
do not give in to them.

Luke 6:22–23

Jesus said, "Blessed are you when men hate you,
when they exclude you and insult you
and reject your name as evil, because of the Son of Man.
Rejoice in that day and leap for joy, because great is your reward in heaven. For that is how their fathers treated the prophets."

※ 2 Peter 2:1–3

But there were also false prophets among the people,
just as there will be false teachers among you. They will
secretly introduce destructive heresies, even denying
the sovereign Lord who bought them—bringing swift
destruction on themselves. Many will follow their
shameful ways and will bring the way of truth into
disrepute. In their greed these teachers will exploit you
with stories they have made up. Their condemnation has
long been hanging over them, and their destruction
has not been sleeping.

perserverance

Imagine wanting something so much that you'd work seven years to get it. (That might be the majority of your life so far!) Don't you think you'd get discouraged after, say, the fourth year or so? But Genesis 29 tells us how Jacob kept going year after year to get what he wanted. He set his eyes on his goal and never gave up. What kind of goals do you have in life? Sports? College? Missions? The key is perseverance—never giving up. Work hard at what God has given you today. That's laying the foundation for what's to come in your future.

✳ James 1:12

Blessed is the man who perseveres under trial, because when he has stood the test, he will receive the crown of life that God has promised to those who love him.

✳ Romans 5:3–4

Not only so, but we also rejoice in our sufferings, because we know that suffering produces perseverance; perseverance, character; and character, hope.

Stake Your
Life on It!

What obstacles are you facing these days? An enemy who's trying to discourage you? A task that seems impossibly big? If you're a believer, you've got a built-in Perseverance Coach, the Holy Spirit, who helps you to keep on keeping on. Keep at it, girl!

James 1:3-4

Because you know that the testing of your faith develops perseverance. Perseverance must finish its work so that you may be mature and complete, not lacking anything.

James 5:11

As you know, we consider blessed those who have persevered. You have heard of Job's perseverance and have seen what the Lord finally brought about. The Lord is full of compassion and mercy.

Romans 2:7

To those who by persistence in doing good seek glory, honor and immortality, he will give eternal life.

John 16:33

Jesus said, "I have told you these things, so that in me you may have peace. In this world you will have trouble. But take heart! I have overcome the world."

Philippians 3:13–14

Brothers, I do not consider myself yet to have taken hold of it. But one thing I do: Forgetting what is behind and straining toward what is ahead, I press on toward the goal to win the prize for which God has called me heavenward in Christ Jesus.

1 Thessalonians 5:24

The one who calls you is faithful and he will do it.

prayer

What do you think prayer is? A list of "thees" and "thous"? Perfectly polished speeches? When Jeremiah poured out his heart to God in the book of Lamentations, he didn't try to impress God with fancy words. Yet his pleas were heartfelt—he rattled off a list of every care and concern on his mind. And he never resorted to whining or disrespect. Believe it or not, God finds that kind of prayer pretty refreshing. He wants you to come to him as you are— not as you think you should be. He wants real communication from the real you. Really.

Stake Your
Life on It!

Prayer is something you learn to do— like most everything else in life. Try some creativity while you practice—journaling your prayers, talking aloud or even singing a praise song to God.

* 2 Chronicles 7:14

If my people, who are called by my name, will humble themselves and pray and seek my face and turn from their wicked ways, then will I hear from heaven and will forgive their sin and will heal their land.

* Philippians 4:6–7

Do not be anxious about anything, but in everything, by prayer and petition, with thanksgiving, present your requests to God. And the peace of God, which transcends all understanding, will guard your hearts and your minds in Christ Jesus.

* Matthew 21:22

Jesus said, "If you believe, you will receive whatever you ask for in prayer."

✳ **James 5:15**

And the prayer offered in faith will make the sick person well; the Lord will raise him up. If he has sinned, he will be forgiven.

✳ **Romans 8:26**

In the same way, the Spirit helps us in our weakness. We do not know what we ought to pray for, but the Spirit himself intercedes for us with groans that words cannot express.

1 Samuel 1:27

I prayed for this child, and the LORD has granted me what I asked of him.

Psalm 6:9

The LORD has heard my cry for mercy;
the LORD accepts my prayer.
Psalm 66:19–20
But God has surely listened
and heard my voice in prayer.
Praise be to God,
who has not rejected my prayer
or withheld his love from me!

pride

Picture this: A "good" Christian girl stands in church and prays, "God, thank you that I'm not like other girls who sleep around, party, smoke, drink and swear— like that tattoo-covered girl over there who'd probably hook up with anyone. What's she doing here?!" Meanwhile, the other girl, who was indeed guilty of all those things, prays tearfully, "God, have mercy on me, a sinner." Now, guess which one makes God smile. Here's a hint: It's not the "good" Christian. It's the one with the humble, repentant heart. That's more important to God than anything else. So, which one are you?

Stake Your
Life on It!

Got a skill or characteristic you're kind of proud of? God wants our pride to rest not in what we have or are, but in him. Are you looking to him or to what's "all that" about you?

* **Psalm 138:6**

Though the LORD is on high, he looks upon the lowly,
*   but the proud he knows from afar.*

* **Proverbs 11:2**

When pride comes, then comes disgrace,
*   but with humility comes wisdom.*

* **Isaiah 2:17**

The arrogance of man will be brought low
*   and the pride of men humbled;*
the LORD alone will be exalted in that day.

* **1 Samuel 2:3**

Do not keep talking so proudly
*   or let your mouth speak such arrogance,*
for the LORD is a God who knows,
*   and by him deeds are weighed.*

* *Isaiah* 13:11

I will punish the world for its evil,
the wicked for their sins.
I will put an end to the arrogance of the haughty
and will humble the pride of the ruthless.

* *Philippians* 3:7–9

But whatever was to my profit I now consider loss for
the sake of Christ. What is more, I consider everything a
loss compared to the surpassing greatness of knowing
Christ Jesus my Lord, for whose sake I have lost all
things. I consider them rubbish, that I may gain Christ
and be found in him, not having a righteousness of my
own that comes from the law, but that which is through
faith in Christ—the righteousness that comes from God
and is by faith.

❋ 1 Corinthians 13:4

Love is patient, love is kind. It does not envy, it does not boast, it is not proud.

❋ 1 Peter 5:5

Young men, in the same way be submissive to those who are older. All of you, clothe yourselves with humility toward one another, because,
"God opposes the proud
   but gives grace to the humble."

purity

When you look in the mirror, what do you see? A pure and holy temple? That's what God sees when he looks at you. Because his Spirit lives in you, that makes you God's temple. Perhaps you don't think very highly of your body, but God does. He's not obsessed with its shape or size. He's not concerned with how trendy your clothes and makeup are. What he does want is for you to guard your purity by taking good care of yourself—for example, staying sexually pure and keeping harmful substances out of your body. That's the least you can do for God's home.

My daughter,

Do you wonder about all the rules in my Word?

It's simple, really. I desire the very best for you.

I want you to be just like me. Holy. Different.

Set apart from those who don't know me. I know that's

a tough assignment, but I'm here to help you.

Your Father

✳ *Titus* 2:11–14

For the grace of God that brings salvation has appeared to all men. It teaches us to say "No" to ungodliness and worldly passions, and to live self-controlled, upright and godly lives in this present age, while we wait for the blessed hope—the glorious appearing of our great God and Savior, Jesus Christ, who gave himself for us to redeem us from all wickedness and to purify for himself a people that are his very own, eager to do what is good.

✳ *1 John* 3:3

Everyone who has this hope in him purifies himself, just as he is pure.

✳ *Psalm* 18:26

To the pure you show yourself pure,
*   but to the crooked you show yourself shrewd.*

* Psalm 119:9

How can a young man keep his way pure?
  By living according to your word.

* Psalm 73:1

Surely God is good to Israel,
  to those who are pure in heart.

* Proverbs 15:26

The LORD detests the thoughts of the wicked,
  but those of the pure are pleasing to him.

* Matthew 5:8

Blessed are the pure in heart,
  for they will see God.

* 2 Corinthians 7:1

Since we have these promises, dear friends, let us purify ourselves from everything that contaminates body and spirit, perfecting holiness out of reverence for God.

Philippians 4:8

Finally, brothers, whatever is true, whatever is noble, whatever is right, whatever is pure, whatever is lovely, whatever is admirable—if anything is excellent or praiseworthy—think about such things.

James 3:17

But the wisdom that comes from heaven is first of all pure; then peace-loving, considerate, submissive, full of mercy and good fruit, impartial and sincere.

Psalm 51:10

Create in me a pure heart, O God,
and renew a steadfast spirit within me.

respect

News Flash: In case you don't already know this, authority figures aren't perfect. And they'd probably be the first to admit it. Yet the Bible tells you to honor them. If you think about it honestly, are you obeying this command? Do you treat your authorities with respect—regardless of how you feel? Do you obey their rules—even when you disagree with them? Your authorities may not be perfect, but God already knows that. And just as he promises, you'll find that obedience brings great rewards.

Stake Your
Life on It!

When you're upset with your leaders, do you talk openly with them about it or complain behind their backs? Hold off on the rebellion until you get an explanation.

✴ Proverbs 11:16

A kindhearted woman gains respect,
but ruthless men gain only wealth.

✴ 1 Peter 3:15

But in your hearts set apart Christ as Lord. Always be
prepared to give an answer to everyone who asks you to
give the reason for the hope that you have. But do this
with gentleness and respect.

✳ *Romans* 12:10

Be devoted to one another in brotherly love. Honor one another above yourselves.

✳ 1 *Peter* 2:17

Show proper respect to everyone: Love the brotherhood of believers, fear God, honor the king.

1 Thessalonians 5:12

Now we ask you, brothers, to respect those
who work hard among you, who are over you
in the Lord and who admonish you.

Romans 13:7

Give everyone what you owe him: If you owe taxes,
pay taxes; if revenue, then revenue; if respect, then
respect; if honor, then honor.

Ephesians 6:1-3

Children, obey your parents in the Lord, for this is right.
"Honor your father and mother"—which is the first
commandment with a promise— "that it may go well
with you and that you may enjoy long life on the earth."

salvation

Being part of a "Christian family" doesn't automatically make you a Christian. Only your own faith in Jesus counts. Do you call yourself a Christian, yet your heart is far from God? Your rightness before God isn't based on how good you are compared to someone else—it's based on whether or not you've placed your faith in Christ's perfect righteousness and his forgiveness. God is far more concerned with your heart than with anything else. Have you experienced the power of God's forgiveness in your life?

Stake Your
Life on It!

Ever heard the phrase "born again"? It means a spiritual rebirth. You can't get into heaven just by living a good life. You have to be spiritually reborn through faith in Christ.

John 3:16

Jesus said, "For God so loved the world that he gave his one and only Son, that whoever believes in him shall not perish but have eternal life."

John 10:9

Jesus said, "I am the gate; whoever enters through me will be saved. He will come in and go out, and find pasture."

Acts 4:12

Salvation is found in no one else, for there is no other name under heaven given to men by which we must be saved.

Mark 16:16

Jesus said, "Whoever believes and is baptized will be saved, but whoever does not believe will be condemned."

Isaiah 45:22

Turn to me and be saved,
all you ends of the earth;
for I am God, and there is no other.

※ **Jeremiah 17:14**

Heal me, O Lord, *and I will be healed;*
  save me and I will be saved,
  for you are the one I praise.

※ **Matthew 10:22**

Jesus said, "All men will hate you because of me, but he who stands firm to the end will be saved."

※ **Acts 2:21**

And everyone who calls
  on the name of the Lord will be saved.

※ **Acts 16:31**

They replied, "Believe in the Lord Jesus, and you will be saved—you and your household."

※ **Romans 10:9–10**

If you confess with your mouth, "Jesus is Lord," and believe in your heart that God raised him from the dead, you will be saved. For it is with your heart that you believe and are justified, and it is with your mouth that you confess and are saved.

Ephesians 2:8

For it is by grace you have been saved, through faith—
and this not from yourselves, it is the gift of God.

Titus 3:5

He saved us, not because of righteous things we had
done, but because of his mercy. He saved us
through the washing of rebirth and renewal by
the Holy Spirit.

Romans 5:9–10

Since we have now been justified by his
blood, how much more shall we be saved
from God's wrath through him! For if, when
we were God's enemies, we were reconciled to
him through the death of his Son, how much
more, having been reconciled, shall we be saved
through his life!

speech

You can tell a lot about a girl by listening to what she says and how she says it. What do your words reveal about you? Do you gush foolish words, say hurtful things and spread lies and gossip? Or do you speak the truth, say helpful things and spread kindness and encouragement? Every time you get ready to open that mouth of yours, think about what you're going to say . . . and what that says about you.

Dear one,

I have given you a great responsibility.

Through you, my child, through your actions, your words,

your attitudes, I will show my holiness to the

world around you. You are the official representative

of my great name. How are you doing?

Sovereign Lord

Ephesians 4:29

Do not let any unwholesome talk come out of your mouths, but only what is helpful for building others up according to their needs, that it may benefit those who listen.

Luke 6:45

Jesus said, "The good man brings good things out of the good stored up in his heart, and the evil man brings evil things out of the evil stored up in his heart. For out of the overflow of his heart his mouth speaks."

Exodus 23:1

Do not spread false reports. Do not help a wicked man by being a malicious witness.

Proverbs 10:19

When words are many, sin is not absent,
but he who holds his tongue is wise.

✳ Proverbs 13:3

He who guards his lips guards his life,
but he who speaks rashly will come to ruin.

✳ James 5:12

Above all, my brothers, do not swear—not by heaven or by earth or by anything else. Let your "Yes" be yes, and your "No," no, or you will be condemned.

✳ Matthew 12:37

Jesus said, "For by your words you will be acquitted, and by your words you will be condemned."

* James 3:10

Out of the same mouth come praise and cursing.
My brothers, this should not be.

* Jeremiah 9:8–9

"Their tongue is a deadly arrow;
*   it speaks with deceit.*
With his mouth each speaks cordially to his neighbor,
*   but in his heart he sets a trap for him.*
Should I not punish them for this?"
*   declares the* LORD.
"Should I not avenge myself
*   on such a nation as this?"*

* Isaiah 6:5–7

"Woe to me!" I cried. "I am ruined! For I am a man of
unclean lips, and I live among a people of unclean lips,
and my eyes have seen the King, the LORD Almighty."

Then one of the seraphs flew to me with a live coal
in his hand, which he had taken with tongs from the
altar. With it he touched my mouth and said, "See, this
has touched your lips; your guilt is taken away and your
sin atoned for."

spiritual growth

As a baby you lived off of milk; it was all that you needed. But now that you've grown, it's important that you have more solid food, such as fruits, veggies, meats, cheeses and breads. When someone first becomes a Christian, she too needs to live off of "just milk" spiritually—just the basics of Christianity. But there comes a time to grow up and move on to more solid food as a follower of Christ—to become a deep learner who uses her spiritual gifts, not just a spiritual baby. How about you? Is it time for you to grow up?

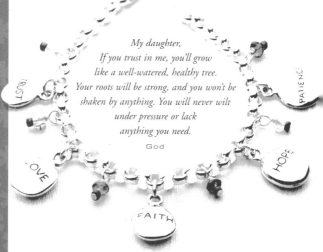

My daughter,
If you trust in me, you'll grow
like a well-watered, healthy tree.
Your roots will be strong, and you won't be
shaken by anything. You will never wilt
under pressure or lack
anything you need.

God

Ephesians 4:12–13

Prepare God's people for works of service, so that the body of Christ may be built up until we all reach unity in the faith and in the knowledge of the Son of God and become mature, attaining to the whole measure of the fullness of Christ.

1 Peter 2:2–3

Like newborn babies, crave pure spiritual milk, so that by it you may grow up in your salvation, now that you have tasted that the Lord is good.

1 Corinthians 3:6–7

I planted the seed, Apollos watered it, but God made it grow. So neither he who plants nor he who waters is anything, but only God, who makes things grow.

Ephesians 4:15

Instead, speaking the truth in love, we will in all things grow up into him who is the Head, that is, Christ.

1 Peter 2:4–5

As you come to him, the living Stone—rejected by men but chosen by God and precious to him— you also, like living stones, are being built into a spiritual house to be a holy priesthood, offering spiritual sacrifices acceptable to God through Jesus Christ.

Isaiah 58:11

The LORD will guide you always;
 he will satisfy your needs in a sun-scorched land
 and will strengthen your frame.
You will be like a well-watered garden,
 like a spring whose waters never fail.

*2 Thessalonians 3:3

But the Lord is faithful, and he will strengthen and protect you from the evil one.

*1 Thessalonians 5:23-24

May God himself, the God of peace, sanctify you through and through. May your whole spirit, soul and body be kept blameless at the coming of our Lord Jesus Christ. The one who calls you is faithful and he will do it.

*Philippians 1:6

Being confident of this, that he who began a good work in you will carry it on to completion until the day of Christ Jesus.

stress

Have you ever had a really bad, horrible, no good, very bad day? Some days all you want to do is curl up in bed and try to forget everything that happened. David had a few days like that—when evil men, enemies and armies were all coming after him. So how did he cope with the fear and stress? He kept his eyes on what mattered most to him: God. When your day takes a sharp turn for the worse, focus on God's faithfulness and power to overcome any problem. And after locking eyes with the Lord, you'll find that you can face the world again—unafraid.

Beloved,

In the midst of your crazy-busy schedule,

in the middle of all your responsibilities and activities,

you can find my peace. Trust in me forever.

I'll keep you in my perfect peace.

The Rock Eternal

Philippians 4:4–7

Rejoice in the Lord always. I will say it again: Rejoice!
Let your gentleness be evident to all. The Lord is near.
Do not be anxious about anything, but in everything,
by prayer and petition, with thanksgiving, present your
requests to God. And the peace of God, which
transcends all understanding, will guard your hearts
and your minds in Christ Jesus.

Isaiah 26:3

You will keep in perfect peace
  him whose mind is steadfast,
  because he trusts in you.

* **Psalm 29:11**

The LORD *gives strength to his people;*
    the LORD *blesses his people with peace.*

* **Isaiah 32:17**

The fruit of righteousness will be peace;
    the effect of righteousness will be quietness and
    confidence forever.

* **Psalm 4:8**

I will lie down and sleep in peace,
    for you alone, O LORD,
    make me dwell in safety.

* **John 16:33**

Jesus said, "I have told you these things, so that in me
you may have peace. In this world you will have trouble.
But take heart! I have overcome the world."

* **2 Corinthians 4:17**

For our light and momentary troubles are achieving for
us an eternal glory that far outweighs them all.

* John 14:27

Jesus said, "Peace I leave with you; my peace I give you. I do not give to you as the world gives. Do not let your hearts be troubled and do not be afraid."

* 1 Peter 5:7

Cast all your anxiety on him because he cares for you.

* Matthew 6:34

Jesus said, "Therefore do not worry about tomorrow, for tomorrow will worry about itself. Each day has enough trouble of its own."

thankfulness

Ingrates. Unappreciative jerks. Losers. In Luke 17 we hear
about how Jesus healed ten lepers, and nine of them
didn't even have the decency to come back and say thank
you. How dare they?! Of course, you'd be the one who
came back to say thanks. Wouldn't you? Because of course
you've thanked God lately—really thanked him with
all your heart—for sending Jesus to die on the cross,
for forgiving your sins, for continuing to love and forgive
you each time you fail him, for giving you strength and joy
to face each day, for the hope of heaven . . . haven't you?

Stake Your
Life on It!

It's easy to say "thanks" with your
mouth without really meaning it.
Real thankfulness involves your time
and effort as well. How can you show
God your thanks?

✱ Psalm 107:1

Give thanks to the LORD, for he is good;
  his love endures forever.

✱ 1 Thessalonians 5:18

Give thanks in all circumstances, for this is God's will for you in Christ Jesus.

✱ Hebrews 12:28

Therefore, since we are receiving a kingdom that cannot be shaken, let us be thankful, and so worship God acceptably with reverence and awe.

✱ Colossians 2:6–7

So then, just as you received Christ Jesus as Lord, continue to live in him, rooted and built up in him, strengthened in the faith as you were taught, and overflowing with thankfulness.

Philippians 4:6

Do not be anxious about anything, but in everything, by prayer and petition, with thanksgiving, present your requests to God.

Deuteronomy 8:10

When you have eaten and are satisfied, praise the LORD your God for the good land he has given you.

Psalm 13:6

I will sing to the LORD,
*   for he has been good to me.*

✳ 1 Chronicles 16:34

Give thanks to the LORD, for he is good;
  his love endures forever.

✳ Psalm 28:7

The LORD is my strength and my shield;
  my heart trusts in him, and I am helped.
My heart leaps for joy
  and I will give thanks to him in song.

✳ Psalm 30:11–12

You turned my wailing into dancing;
  you removed my sackcloth and clothed me with joy,
that my heart may sing to you and not be silent.
  O LORD my God, I will give you thanks forever.

wisdom

We often associate wisdom with old age, like the wise old owl and the wizened white-haired professor. We make the mistake of thinking that you can't really be wise till you're way older. While it's true that wisdom often comes from experience, you can also become wise by doing several things: accepting advice from your parents, following God's commands and actively seeking wisdom. The Lord promises to give wisdom to those who go after it (James 1:5).

*My child,
I've given you the most valuable
source of wisdom you'll ever find—
my Word. It's your guide to living,
your key to success,
your path to a rich and full life.
Write my Word on your heart.
You won't be sorry.*

The living Word

James 1:5

If any of you lacks wisdom, he should ask God, who gives generously to all without finding fault, and it will be given to him.

Proverbs 8:10–11

Choose my instruction instead of silver,
*   knowledge rather than choice gold,*
for wisdom is more precious than rubies,
*   and nothing you desire can compare with her.*

Proverbs 1:7

The fear of the LORD is the beginning of knowledge,
*   but fools despise wisdom and discipline.*

* James 3:17

But the wisdom that comes from heaven is first of all pure; then peace-loving, considerate, submissive, full of mercy and good fruit, impartial and sincere.

* Psalm 119:98

Your commands make me wiser than my enemies,
for they are ever with me.

* Proverbs 2:6

For the LORD gives wisdom,
and from his mouth come knowledge and understanding.

* Proverbs 2:10–11

For wisdom will enter your heart,
and knowledge will be pleasant to your soul.
Discretion will protect you,
and understanding will guard you.

* Proverbs 13:10

Pride only breeds quarrels,
but wisdom is found in those who take advice.

❊ Proverbs 4:7

Wisdom is supreme; therefore get wisdom.
Though it cost all you have, get understanding.

❊ James 3:13

Who is wise and understanding among you? Let him show it by his good life, by deeds done in the humility that comes from wisdom.

❊ Matthew 7:24–25

Jesus said, "Therefore everyone who hears these words of mine and puts them into practice is like a wise man who built his house on the rock. The rain came down, the streams rose, and the winds blew and beat against that house; yet it did not fall, because it had its foundation on the rock."

witnessing

You want to have beautiful feet? Spiritually speaking, a pedicure just won't do it. Nope, the way to beautiful feet is through taking them to different places and sharing the good news about Jesus. Take them to your classes, to cheerleading practice, to work, to the mall, to the movies, to the coffee house, to your aunt's house, to your friend's house, to your house. . . . Being able to share God's message of love and mercy to the lost is a beautiful thing. So get walking!

Stake Your Life on It!

So you might not be able to recite the Bible by memory or debate theology with famous gurus. Okay. Just be ready to share your faith when you get an opportunity. A Christian who lives with integrity and consistency will gain others' respect and a voice to share Christ with them.

Matthew 5:14–16

Jesus said, "You are the light of
the world. A city on a hill cannot be
hidden. Neither do people light a lamp
and put it under a bowl. Instead they put it on
its stand, and it gives light to everyone in the house.
In the same way, let your light shine before men,
that they may see your good deeds and praise your
Father in heaven."

John 15:26–27

Jesus said, "When the Counselor comes, whom I will
send to you from the Father, the Spirit of truth who
goes out from the Father, he will testify about me.
And you also must testify, for you have been with me
from the beginning."

Romans 1:16

I am not ashamed of the gospel, because it is the power
of God for the salvation of everyone who believes: first
for the Jew, then for the Gentile.

* 1 Peter 3:15

But in your hearts set apart Christ as Lord. Always be prepared to give an answer to everyone who asks you to give the reason for the hope that you have. But do this with gentleness and respect.

* Mark 13:11

Jesus said, "Whenever you are arrested and brought to trial, do not worry beforehand about what to say. Just say whatever is given you at the time, for it is not you speaking, but the Holy Spirit."

* Acts 23:11

The following night the Lord stood near Paul and said, "Take courage! As you have testified about me in Jerusalem, so you must also testify in Rome."

✳ Matthew 28:18–20

Then Jesus came to them and said, "All authority in heaven and on earth has been given to me. Therefore go and make disciples of all nations, baptizing them in the name of the Father and of the Son and of the Holy Spirit, and teaching them to obey everything I have commanded you. And surely I am with you always, to the very end of the age."

✳ 2 Corinthians 4:1–5

Therefore, since through God's mercy we have this ministry, we do not lose heart. Rather, we have renounced secret and shameful ways; we do not use deception, nor do we distort the word of God. On the contrary, by setting forth the truth plainly we commend ourselves to every man's conscience in the sight of God. And even if our gospel is veiled, it is veiled to those who are perishing. The god of this age has blinded the minds of unbelievers, so that they cannot see the light of the gospel of the glory of Christ, who is the image of God. For we do not preach ourselves, but Jesus Christ as Lord, and ourselves as your servants for Jesus' sake.

the covenant

Above all else, guard your heart,
for it is the wellspring of life.

Proverbs 4:23

What does it mean to be a True Images girl?

- ✳ A True Images girl knows what she wants. She's willing to give up what the world has to offer since it will never make her truly happy. Because God designed her, only he can make her complete and her life full (John 10:10).

- ✳ A True Images girl guards her mind. She protects her mental purity from destructive images in the media and commits to filling her mind with what is pure and true (Philippians 4:8).

- ✳ A True Images girl is willing to wait. She values her sexual purity, trusting that God's plan is best

and that he will bless those who are obedient to him (Psalm 1:1–3).

✳ A True Images girl has genuine beauty. She doesn't seek shallow outer beauty; she desires a deep, inner, lasting beauty (Proverbs 31:30).

✳ A True Images girl is true to herself. She develops qualities of genuine character, such as love, contentment, kindness, self-control, integrity and purity (Galatians 5:22–23).

✳ A True Images girl looks for leaders. She models her life after the women of God, those in the Bible and those in her own church (Hebrews 13:7).

✳ A True Images girl knows her worth. She knows that her personal value is not based on her appearance, performance, popularity or accomplishments but on who she is in God's eyes (Psalm 139:13–16).

✳ A True Images girl's first love is Jesus. Knowing he passionately and deeply loves her changes how she lives her life (1 John 3:1).

✳ A True Images girl is a girl of the Word. She stays connected to God through reading the Bible and growing her roots deep into Christ (Colossians 2:6–7).

＊   A True Images girl gives away her faith.
She knows the secret to eternal life, and she
shares that freely with others who need God
(Galatians 6:9).

＊   A True Images girl is never alone. She knows that
there are other girls out there who are striving to
live for Christ just as she is
(Romans 12:4–5).

A True Images girl makes a statement—not about
what she does or does not do—but about who she is.
If you want to be a True Images girl,
   Take your stand.
      Embrace the covenant.
         Be true.

christianity 101

Perhaps the greatest mystery of life is that the Creator of the universe loves you. He spins the galaxies and directs the course of history, yet he also wants to have a personal relationship with you. He wants to be closer to you than your parents, a best friend or even a boyfriend.

First, some bad news.

Not only does God exist, but he's also holy. That means he's perfect. He's never made a mistake or done something he's regretted. He's never been guilty of a crime or broken a law. In short, God is free from any hint of sin. He's so holy and perfect that someone who sins can't even stand in his presence. Even worse news for us is that sin must be paid for—and the price is high. God said that the "wages of sin is death" (Romans 6:23) and that "without the shedding of blood there is no forgiveness" (Hebrews 9:22). Sin is serious. The Old Testament describes how the Hebrew people offered sacrifices of lambs and goats to make payment for their sins (see Leviticus 1—7).

Second, some good news.

After thousands of years of sacrifices, God provided a better way. God sent his Son, Jesus Christ, as the perfect

Lamb. Jesus was both fully God and fully human. As God, he was perfect in every way. As a man, he knows what it's like to be us. He experienced the same temptations we experience, and he represents us before God at all times. He died on the cross for us (Matthew 27:32–61). Proving he had power over all sin and death, he didn't stay dead. After three days he was raised to life again (Matthew 28). Because he was without fault and sin, he was the perfect sacrifice—a sacrifice so complete that it's powerful enough to forgive all your sins—past, present and future (Hebrews 10:17–18).

Jesus paid the penalty we deserve for our sins. In exchange, he gives us his righteousness. In other words, when God sees us, he doesn't see our sin any more; he sees Jesus' holiness, which has been given to us (2 Corinthians 5:17–21).

So, what's Christianity?

Simply put, Christianity is aligning yourself with Christ.

* It's admitting that you have sinned and that your sin is really offensive to God (Psalm 53:3).

* It's recognizing that there's nothing you can do yourself to pay for your sins (Romans 3:23).

✳ It's confessing your sins to God. Even though he already knows them, he wants us to confess them—to come to grips with them (1 John 1:9).

✳ It's following him—getting to know him, reading his Word and doing your best to follow him daily (Romans 12:1–2).

So, what's next?

If you'd like to become a follower of Christ and enjoy friendship with God, here's a great way to get started.

Pray.

Here's a prayer that can help you give your life to Jesus:

God, I believe in you. I know that I am a sinner. Thank you for sending your Son, Jesus, to die for my sins and make me right with you. Please come into my life. I give it to you. I want to live for you from now on.

Read.

Spend some regular time getting to know God better. Read some of God's Word each day. Spend some time thinking about what you read and talking with God. Tell him about your day, the things you're learning, the things that frustrate you and the things that you're excited about. As a true friend, he cares about you and your life.

Don't go it alone.

The Christian life isn't meant to be lived alone.

Spend time with other Christians.
Get involved in a church or youth group
that loves God and wants you to know
him better.
Remember . . .
Above all else, remember that God's friendship with
you is permanent. Sure, there will be times when you
make mistakes. You'll fail, you'll sin, and you'll even feel
guilty. There will be times when you disappoint yourself
and others. In those moments, though, remember that
God is your constant companion. He remains your proud
friend, loving Father and faithful Savior. He'll never leave
you; he'll never forsake you. He promises you that
(Romans 8:28–39).

If you've recently become a Christian,
we'd love to hear your story. Log on
to www.TrueImagesBible.com, click
on the "Tell Us Your Story" link and
tell us when and how you decided to
follow Christ.

30-day READING PLAN
30 Days of Genuine Living

At Inspirio we love to hear from you—
your stories, your feedback,
and your product ideas.
Please send your comments to us
by way of e-mail at
icares@zondervan.com
or to the address below:

inspirio

Attn: Inspirio Cares
5300 Patterson Avenue SE
Grand Rapids, MI 49530

If you would like further information
about Inspirio and the products we
create please visit us at:
www.inspiriogifts.com

Thank you and God Bless!